BOOK 3

T0050964

REVISED EDITION

Tunes You Like

Your Favorite Songs Made Easy to Play

Arranged For Piano Solo By
Mark Nevin

CONTENTS

American Patrol 17
Arkansas Traveler 15
Billy Boy 6
Blue Danube Waltz 23
Camptown Races 8
Clementine 13
Home Sweet Home 14
I've Been Workin' On The Railroad 10
Joy To The World 16
Melody In F 7
Merry Widow Waltz 21
My Bonnie 11
Oh, How Lovely Is The Evening 12
Old Gray Mare, The 2
On Top Of Old Smoky 22
Pop! Goes The Weasel 9
Prayer Of Thanksgiving 20
Reveille 4
Sailing, Sailing 19
Sailor's Hornpipe 18
Skip To My Lou 5
Taps 3

G. SCHIRMER, Inc.

DISTRIBUTED BY
HAL•LEONARD®
CORPORATION
7777 W. BLUEMOUND RD. P.O. BOX 13819 MILWAUKEE, WI 53213

The Old Grey Mare

American Folk Song
Arranged by Mark Nevin

The old grey mare she ain't what she used to be,

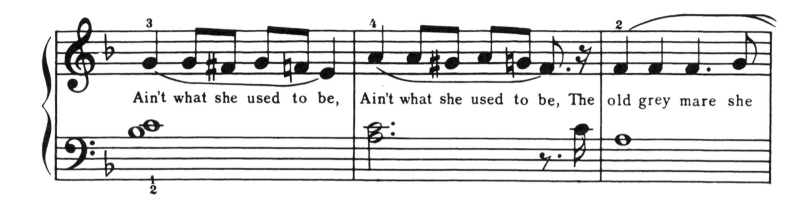

Ain't what she used to be, Ain't what she used to be, The old grey mare she

ain't what she used to be Man-y long years a - go. Oh,

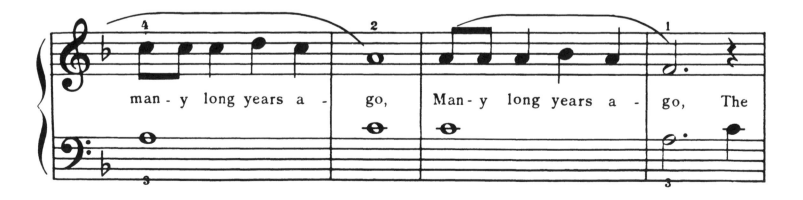

man-y long years a - go, Man-y long years a - go, The

old grey mare she ain't what she used to be, Ain't what she used to be,

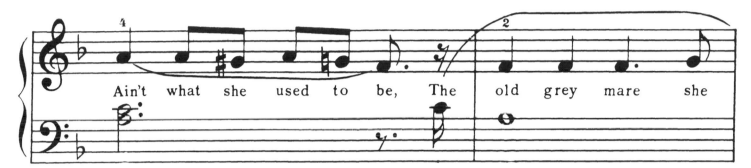

Ain't what she used to be, The old grey mare she

ain't what she used to be, Man-y long years a go

Taps

U.S. Army Bugle Call
Arranged by Mark Nevin

Moderato

mp Day is done, gone the sun from the hills, from the sky All is

well safe-ly rest, safe-ly rest, God is nigh

Reveille

U. S. Army Bugle Call
Arranged by Mark Nevin

Moderato

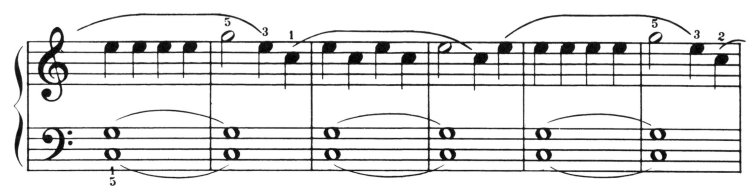

Skip to My Lou

Traditional Folk Song
Arranged by Mark Nevin

Choose your part-ners, skip to my Lou, choose your part-ners, skip to my Lou,

Choose your part-ners, skip to my Lou, skip to my Lou, my dar - lin'.

Round and round and skip to my Lou, round and round and skip to my Lou,

Round and round and skip to my Lou, skip to my Lou, my dar - lin'.

Billy Boy

American Folk Song
Arranged by Mark Nevin

Moderato

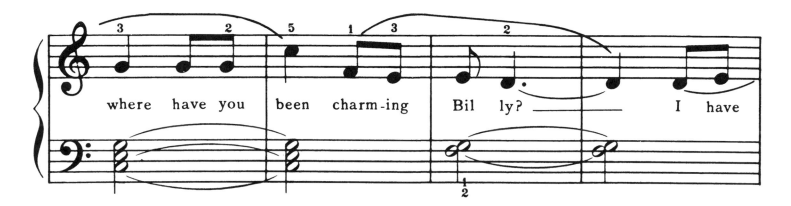

Melody in F

Anton Rubinstein
Arranged by Mark Nevin

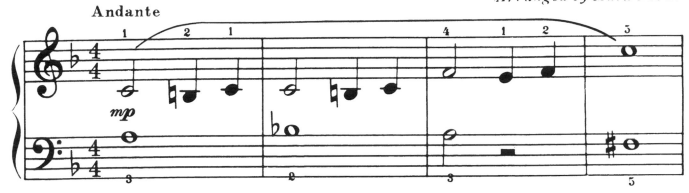

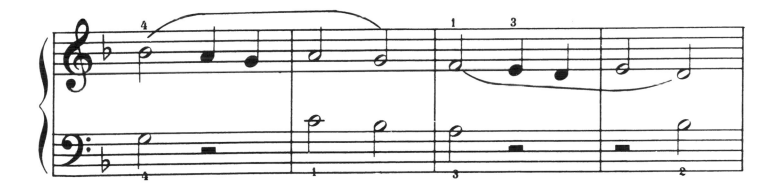

Camptown Races

Stephen Foster
Arranged by Mark Nevin

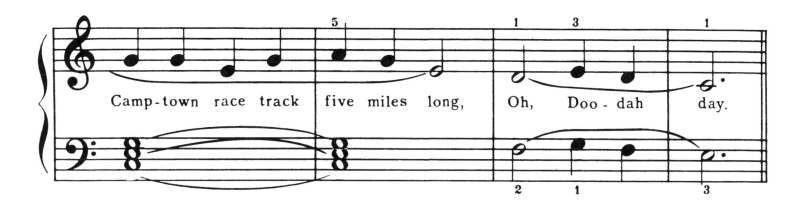

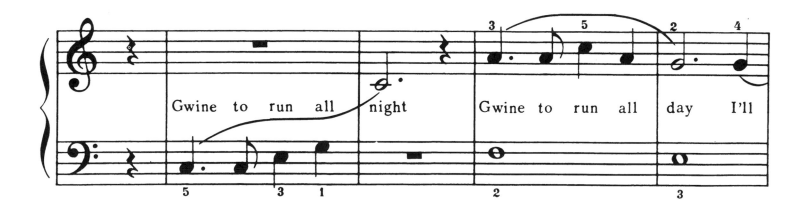

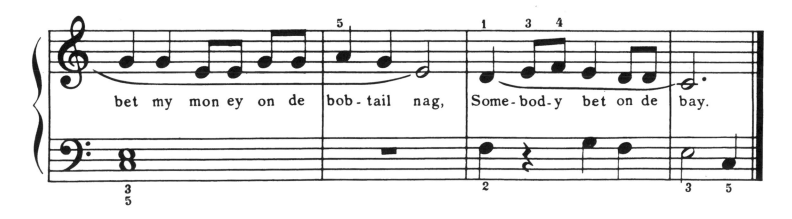

Pop! Goes the Weasel

American Folk Tune
Arranged by Mark Nevin

I've Been Workin' on the Railroad

Arranged by Mark Nevin

I've been work-in' on the rail-road all the live-long day.

I've been work-in' on the rail-road to pass the time a - way

Don't you hear the whis-tle blow-in' rise so ear-ly in the morn

Don't you hear the cap-tain shout-in' "Din - ah, blow your horn."

My Bonnie

Arranged by Mark Nevin

Oh, How Lovely Is the Evening

Arranged by Mark Nevin

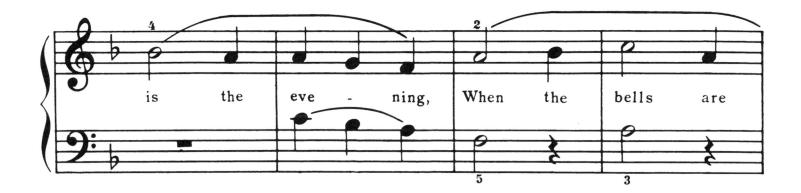

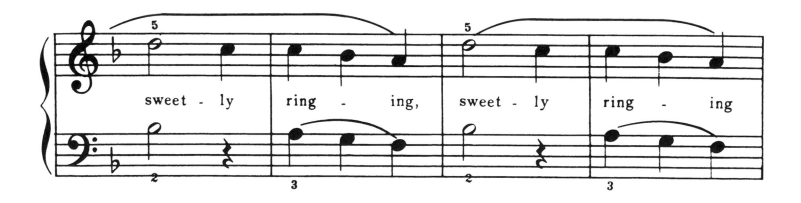

Clementine

Moderato

Arranged by Mark Nevin

In a cav - ern, in a can - yon, ex - ca - vat - ing for a

mine, Dwelt a min - er for - ty nin - er and his daugh - ter Clem - en -

tine. Oh my dar - ling, Oh my dar - ling, Oh my dar - ling Clem - en -

tine, You are lost and gone for - ev - er dread - ful sor - ry Clem - en - tine.

Home, Sweet Home

Henry R. Bishop
Arranged by Mark Nevin

Andantino

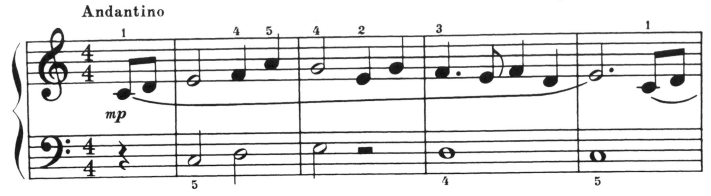

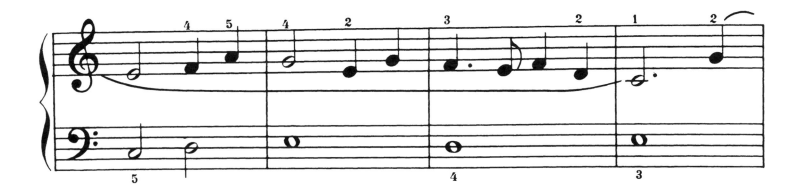

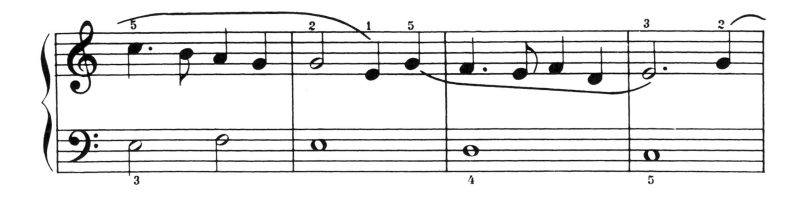

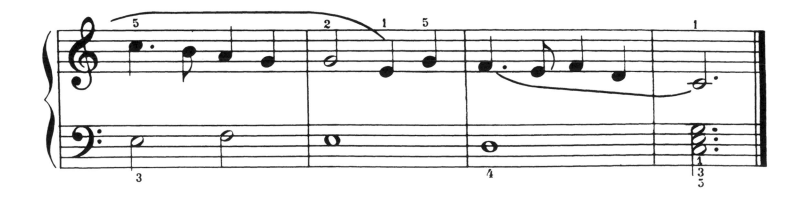

Arkansas Traveler

American Folk Tune
Arranged by Mark Nevin

Lively

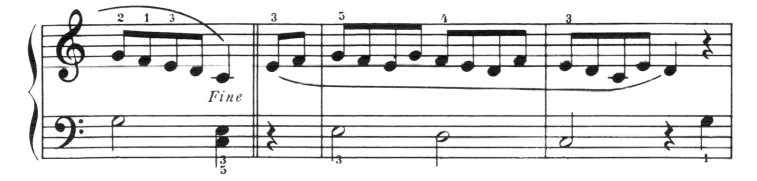

Joy to the World

George F. Handel
Arranged by Mark Nevin

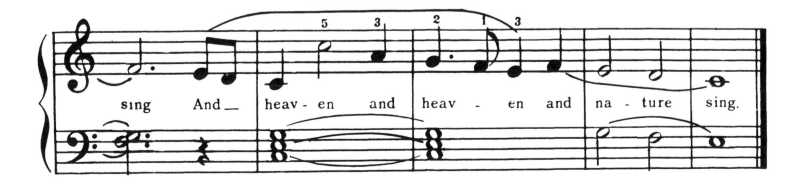

American Patrol

F. W. Meacham
Arranged by Mark Nevin

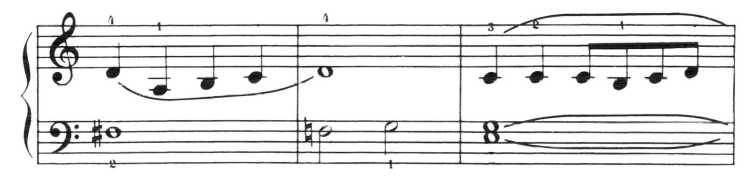

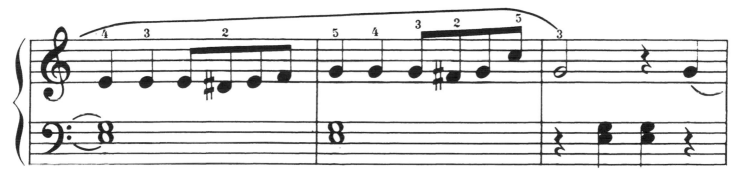

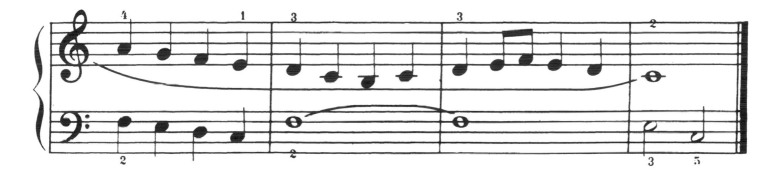

Sailor's Hornpipe

Lively

Arranged by Mark Nevin

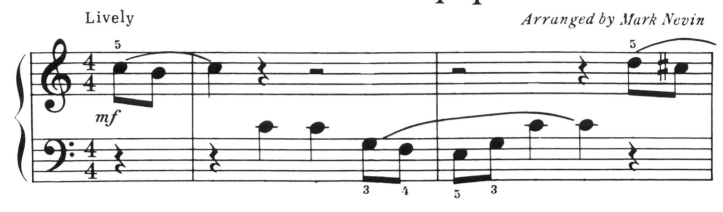

Sailing, Sailing

Moderato

Arranged by Mark Nevin

mf Sail - ing, sail - ing o - ver the bound-ing main_____ For

man - y a storm - y wind shall blow ere Jack comes home a - gain.____

Sail - ing, sail - ing o - ver the bound-ing main_____ For

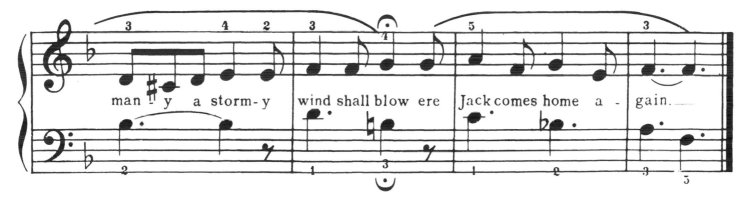

man - y a storm - y wind shall blow ere Jack comes home a - gain.

Prayer of Thanksgiving

Dutch Folk Song
Words and Arrangement by Mark Nevin

Andantino

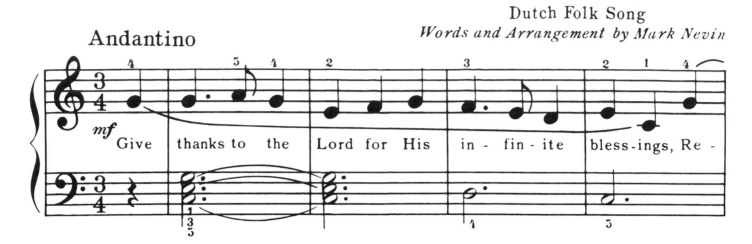

Give thanks to the Lord for His in - fin - ite bless - ings, Re -

joice that we live in this land of the free, Let's

gath - er to - geth - er and sanc - ti - fy our bless - ings, Sing

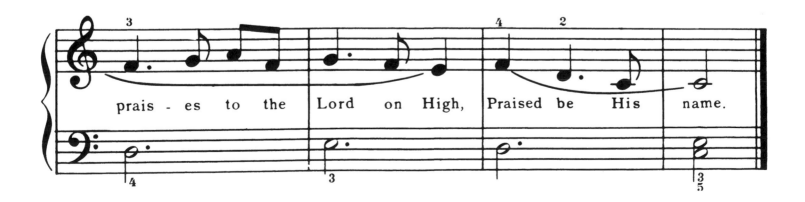

prais - es to the Lord on High, Praised be His name.

Merry Widow Waltz

Franz Lehar
Arranged by Mark Nevin

Tempo di Valse

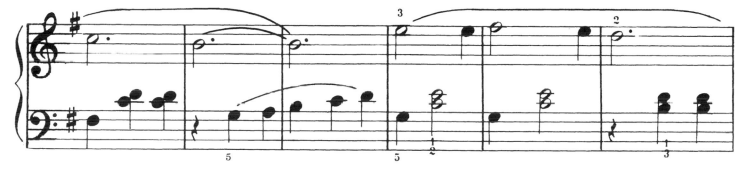

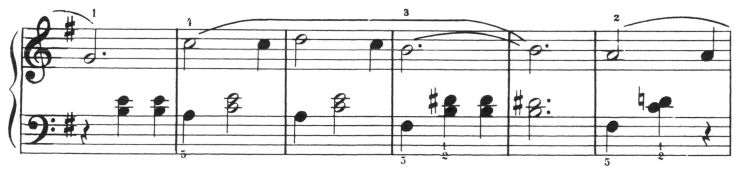

On Top of Old Smoky

American Folk Song
Arranged by Mark Nevin

Blue Danube Waltz

Johann Strauss
Arranged by Mark Nevin

Tempo di Valse

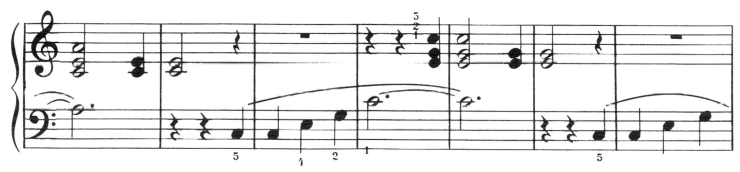

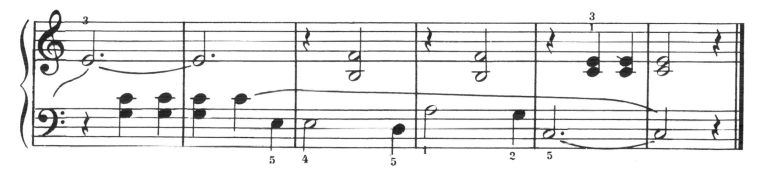